UNDERSTANDING KUNG FU

DEMYSTIFYING TRADITIONAL CONCEPTS

SHKAR SHARIF

ACKNOWLEDGMENTS

I am thankful to my numerous teachers across the different traditions and systems for being so generous with their knowledge.

I am thankful to my students, who allow me to make a living from what I love.

I want to give specific thanks to two of my students: Darina Dimitrova for her fantastic illustrations for this book; and Dolan O'Toole for his detailed read through and advice.

Finally, none of this would be possible without my wife, Kristina. She removes life's many obstacles, allowing me to train, write and teach.

If there is anything of use in this book, the thanks are due to my teachers, who taught me well, and, if anything falls short, it is due to my own shortcomings. I am always learning and will do better in future.

CONTENTS

INTRODUCTION

At one point or another during childhood, most parents decide that it is good to take their children to martial arts classes; my parents were no different. The first memory of any martial arts I have was attending a judo class when I was six. I vaguely recall being surrounded by a large group of children wearing the traditional white judo gi, while I was in shorts and a T-shirt. I remember being pushed by one of the more experienced boys, and this scared me. I had never been in any form of physical altercation, and the thought that this boy could hurt me gave me a real shock. It was so long ago that I don't recall much more of the event, but I remember my parents not taking me back to the class, probably because I was too scared to go back.

One of my younger cousins was a very active boy. It often felt like he could not go a single day without getting into trouble for breaking things or hitting other children. His parents, my uncle and aunt, thought that it might be a good idea to start him in karate classes. The thinking was that karate lessons might help direct his hyperactivity and give him some discipline. He had been attending karate classes for a couple of weeks when he started showing off to us about what he was learning. True to form, I started bugging my parents about letting me go to karate classes. Again, our parents gave in to our requests, signing my brother and I up to one of the local Wado-ryu karate schools.

Karate classes were fun. I was older, around the age of ten, and was not afraid of fighting anymore. Like all older boys I got into my fair share of scrapes with my brothers and with other children at school. The class was an hour long, between thirty and forty of us learning katas, practising specific techniques, and my favourite, sparring. Our teacher, Sensei Brian, was a lovely man. He was very patient with us and pushed us in class. I often look back on these classes with my brothers, and we reminisce how, at the end of the class, Sensei would make us hold painful stances. Without fail, about ten of us suddenly needed to be excused at the same time, as we needed to use the toilet. We would stand outside the hall and laugh and joke, proud of ourselves, thinking that we were so smart because we had cheated Sensei; not knowing that the only people we had cheated were ourselves.

Eventually, I found the martial art I was destined for in my mid-teens. A school friend had started training in a local kung fu school and asked me to come along to try a class. The kung fu system was Tiger Crane Combination; a style heavily influenced by Southern Yong Chun White Crane, with a flavour of Taizuquan, or Grand Ancestor Fist. In addition to this, I began learning a rare white crane system called Shuang Yang Quan. Shuang Yang Quan is practised slowly and mindfully like Taijiquan; Taijiquan being a Daoist system and Shuang Yang being a Chan Buddhist system out of Shaolin. The whole system consists of sixty-six postures woven together to make the form.

Broadly speaking, traditional Chinese kung fu can be

divided into two categories: external styles and internal styles. These two descriptions have been interpreted in different ways throughout history and have meant different things to different people. One of the more interesting accounts of the external and internal styles of kung fu can be traced back to the divide between Shaolin and Wudang Kung Fu. Wudang Kung Fu was developed by Daoist priests living on Wudang Mountain in Hubei Province. With Daoism being an indigenous Chinese religion, Wudang Kung Fu was referred to as an internal style. By contrast, Shaolin Kung Fu was a product of Buddhist monks. Buddhism, being an import from India, was referred to as an external style. More commonly, kung fu systems that use the mind to mobilise the relaxed body, in accordance to Daoist principles, are referred to as internal systems, and kung fu systems that are more explosive and use strength are known as external. I personally disagree with this distinction as I believe that all kung fu systems must begin on the outside and become more and more internal.

I began teaching these systems relatively young; probably a little too young. I opened my first kung fu club in 2006, under the guidance of my then instructor, and, in 2014, my wife and I opened our current club Kung Fu Zone. I have taught hundreds of students in the past sixteen years and have seen first hand how training truly transforms people's lives. I have also seen how expectations and outlooks in younger students today differs from my own when I began training.

Over the last decade, conservative institutions have been forced to take a long hard look at their core tenets and how they do things. Traditional martial arts are not immune to these seismic societal shifts. A new generation of people born after the boom years are realising that the old order does not work for them and that they will probably be less well off than their parents. These younger people are losing faith in institutions and long-standing traditions at an unprecedented scale. "It has always been that way", or "Because my teacher said so" are no longer being accepted as reasons for continuing to do things in the traditional way. People need to know why things are done in this way and expect to see tangible results quickly.

A harmful reaction to the loss of trust in long-standing institutions and traditions is the breakdown of social cohesion. Whether in our politics, our spiritual traditions or our martial arts people are becoming increasingly tribal. Within the martial arts world, the 'my school is better than your school' mentality has always existed, but the internet and social media have further deepened these divisions. Sports martial artists blame traditional martial arts for not evolving and for using outdated techniques that are not practical. On the other hand, traditional martial artists accuse sports martial arts of co-opting techniques from traditional systems into rule-based competitions and claiming them as their own and as being superior.

Another big problem with the traditional martial arts world is the development of the martial arts 'cult'; schools run by an infallible master, who is not to be questioned. This kind of person surrounds himself with junior instructors to control students and uses high-pressure selling techniques and character assassinations on any student who doesn't conform. These kinds of schools isolate themselves from the wider martial arts community because cult leaders always like to work in darkness, away from the glare of those who can hold them to account. Students looking for spiritual meaning and guidance in an increasingly material and atheistic world are attracted to these schools. They follow these authority figures with blind faith, never questioning them and taking what is told to them as gospel.

One recurring theme that I come across again and again in the kung fu community is a lack of depth of knowledge of underlying principles. This is not surprising; the traditions that gave rise to these kung fu systems are esoteric and shrouded in mystery.

Bodhidharma, the legendary patriarch of Shaolin Kung Fu, is credited with establishing the Chan/Zen branch of Mahayana Buddhism. He developed the Yi Jin Jing exercises to give the monks a robust and resilient body so that they could have the stamina to withstand the physical toll of hours of meditation. In the same vein, the legendary founder of taijiquan, Zhang Sanfeng, was a Daoist sage and is purported to have been a master of Daoyin, the Daoist internal arts.

It can be challenging for Chinese martial arts practitioners with no experience of these traditions to truly appreciate the level of complexity contained in often contradictory sounding instructions. These poetic and mystical statements are often disregarded by teachers and students, treating them as archaic remnants of an irrelevant philosophy or religion that doesn't matter in the 21st century. For all the advances humanity has made over the centuries, our understanding of our own internal state and the reality we occupy has regressed. Now, more than ever, we need to understand what we are and how to cultivate internal and external change.

Those of us who train in traditional kung fu disciplines very quickly become acquainted with words like 'Qi', 'Song', 'Jin', 'Shen', 'Yi' and 'Yin Yang'. But how many of you actually understand what these words or concepts mean practically? How many of you know how to begin implementing them into your training today?

I have written this book as an antidote to this lack of depth of knowledge. Kung fu is full of practical wisdom on how to change our bodies and minds to become something better. I believe that these lessons should not be hidden behind language that can often be indecipherable to those who have not grown up in the cultures of the East.

In Part 1 of the book, I have broken down the key terms and ideas that a traditional Chinese martial artist may come across during their first decade of training. I have attempted to explain what each term means and how you can utilise each concept. In Part 2 of the book, I give some essential exercises that you can use to achieve some level of foundational skill in Chinese martial arts. These exercises are ones I have trained in myself and teach to my students to help them build their foundation.

One last point I want to clarify is that the kung fu principles and concepts outlined in this book are multilayered and mean different things at different levels of attainment. Generally speaking, the principles become less gross and more refined, making their way from the physical towards emptiness. The more we all train, the more we peel away the layers. But to get anywhere worth going we need to begin engaging with the physical world because this is where we find ourselves. In my view, traditional Chinese martial arts is a path to solving the greatest mysteries of existence, by beginning with what we have here now: our bodies.

I

THEORY

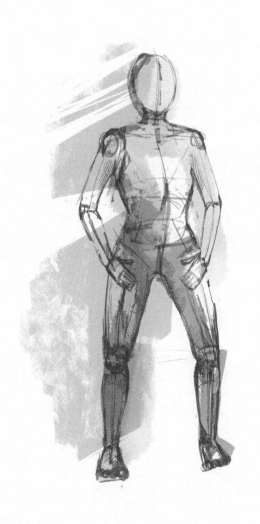

1

JIBENGONG – LAYING THE FOUNDATION

*B*efore I get into terms and breakdown concepts, I want to clarify what traditional Chinese martial arts is about and how it develops and changes a practitioner. Unlike most modern martial arts, where the focus is on drilling and learning techniques, traditional Chinese martial arts is about changing the body and the mind. Jibengong or foundation training is taught from the beginning to students because developing the correct body is paramount. Yes, the external shapes and movements may look like kung fu, but without the proper internal development from foundation training. The thing being practised is kung fu in name only. Different traditions have different ways of teaching students foundation training. Zhan Zhuang, Yi Jin Jing, some forms of Ba Duan Jin, and San Zhan or Sum Chien from Southern Shaolin are very effective foundation training methods that have proven their ability to create the required transformations over time.

Chinese kung fu attempts to deal with force and create force by bypassing the muscles and using the whole body instead of just the limb or surrounding area. Suppose we consider a straight punch that exists in all striking arts. When doing a correct kung fu punch, the arm doing the punch is usually only a final expression of the movement. The punch begins at the waist, connects to the ground and comes back up into the fist. Foundation training develops the pathways and structure required for the journey that the kinetic energy makes. Without foundation training, a punch is just an arm movement. Some modern arts have started understanding this. Modern boxing, for example, has understood the effectiveness in using the whole body in a similar way to kung fu systems. Some boxing coaches teach a process called the kinetic chain, which encourages the body's connection through the joints to power the punch.

Further to this, kung fu aims to develop mind and body integration. Foundation training helps the body, deformed over years by bad habits and incorrect movement, find alignment, loosen and open. It does this by training awareness and intention. The mind becomes intimately aware of the body, knowing every inch. The average person cannot differentiate between their bones, their muscles and their tendons. Everything feels like a solid mass. Somebody who has undergone correct foundation training will be able to distinguish between these separate parts of the body. They will then be able to direct and control individual parts of a small area of the body.

The process of changing the body also changes the mind. The training allows the mind to expand its ability to be aware and to know. The mind seeps deeper and deeper into the body, helping the practitioner understand their body. Eventually, the body becomes a tool commanded entirely by the mind. This development of the mind's ability to know does not only go inwards; it expands outwards also. On contact with an opponent, the practitioner knows the opponent's body just as well as they know their own.

Every practitioner must go through different stages of development when training in traditional Chinese martial arts.

The first stage is the stage of forms and shapes. A student must learn the specific shapes, movements and physical structures that the particular system they have chosen teaches. They must change the physical body so that the forms and shapes are not forced and can be settled into with ease; taking them to a stage where the system's shapes and structures become the intuitive way in which they move and stand. Thought is no longer needed to align correctly; the body structure is intuitively correct. These shapes can be like external scaffolding that allows the student to enter inside and do the next stage of work.

With the body now aligned correctly and holding the body structure in place, the student moves inside and begins the long and challenging process of changing the internal. This process is not about adding anything – it is purely a process of letting go and abandoning all that is unnecessary. We build up a lifetime of bad habits, ways of thinking, emotional states, and these all directly affect how our body and energy move and react. The work at this stage is about letting go physically and mentally of all that offers resistance. The first five to ten years of training have given us the scaffolding and structures physically and mentally so that we don't crumble during this process of abandoning the unnecessary. Attainment during this stage of training depends less on the quantity of training than the quality of one's training. This part of training is challenging and is very difficult to navigate without a good teacher who knows the path through experience.

The final stage is about removing the scaffolding. The structures and shapes the student has mastered no longer matter. Internal and external are no longer separate, and all things are united. In essence, the whole journey is about learning how to do, so that we can abandon doing.

This need for complete transformation is one of the main reasons why mastery or proficiency in the traditional martial arts is spoken of in decades and lifetimes. Yes, it is possible to learn all the forms and techniques of any given system within a few years. Yes, it is possible to learn to fight and win competitions within a few years. If that is all that you are after, fair enough. But, if you are after complete transformation of your body and mind, you need to dedicate your life to the art. It is not surprising then that a practitioner within their first ten years of training believes that they have high skill but, the more they train beyond this, the less confident they are at their skill level.

2

WHAT IS QI?

Over the centuries, Qi has been described by Chinese philosophers, martial artists and internal alchemists in different ways; breath and energy being the two main descriptions that we see. Many kung fu practitioners will tell anyone who listens about Qi energy being the source of their skill, without really exploring or trying to understand this further; satisfied by what they have been told through their specific tradition. This lack of intellectual exploration can lead practitioners down a path of confirmation bias. On the flip side, beginners can often feel frustrated and unsatisfied because these descriptions don't provide practical explanations of how and why, and can cause a sceptic to throw out the baby with the bathwater. Concluding that, if no one can explain this to me in logical terms, then it must all be rubbish.

The concept of Qi can mean different things within the various branches of traditional Chinese systems. Qi within traditional Chinese medicine can be very different from the concept of Qi discussed in Nei Gong: the Chinese internal cultivation arts. Within the traditional Chinese martial arts alone, the concept of Qi can be used in several different ways. It is not uncommon to hear kung fu teachers telling their students to "breath in the Qi", "sink your Qi" or "lead the Qi to your extremities when you strike." It is not uncommon for students to nod along as if this statement has made perfect sense, when, in reality, the students and, unfortunately, sometimes the teacher also have no clue what they are talking about.

My own relationship with Qi was unbalanced during my early days of training as a teenager. I was certain that, if I could only understand and use this wondrous supernatural energy, I would be like the heroes I watched in kung fu movies. To my then teacher's credit, he noticed this in me and would call me a hippy every time I talked about Qi and encouraged me to get good at the basics, and the rest will come.

I do not know enough about traditional Chinese medicine to discuss the uses of Qi within that paradigm. I will leave that for more capable minds to explain. My explanation of Qi is strictly within the kung fu paradigm and should not be superimposed on other systems that use Qi.

Traditional kung fu systems all use Qi as a root principle and the concept of Qi can be found dotted all over classical texts like the Taiji classics.

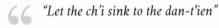

"Let the ch'i sink to the dan-t'ien"

— (THE TREATISE ON T'AI CHI CHU'UAN
ATTRIBUTED TO WANG TSUNG-YUEH [WANG
ZONGYUE] (18TH CENTURY), AS RESEARCHED BY LEE
N SCHEELE)

There are many other references to Qi within these texts, all explaining what Qi is, how to cultivate it and how to use it. The only issue is that these texts were written by masters who had achieved these levels themselves, so were describing these processes subjectively. It's almost impossible for a beginner to understand what these texts are describing without achieving a similar level and having the proverbial light bulb go off in their own heads, through subjective experience.

Within the Chinese martial arts, the word 'Qi' is usually not used as a noun; it is used as a verb. The word is often not describing one thing, like energy or breath (although on occasions it can). Qi is usually a word describing several processes that are occurring. All movement in the body must be as a result of muscles. Generally speaking, there are two types of muscles: the voluntary muscle system and the involuntary muscle system. The voluntary muscles are the muscles such as our biceps and diaphragm that we can control with our will and intent. The involuntary muscles are the muscles such as our cardiac muscle and the muscles around our organs controlled by the autonomous nervous system. At first glance, we seem to have no direct control over these involuntary muscles.

What if there is a way to have a degree of control over some of these involuntary muscle systems? Take the arrector pili muscles: the small muscles on our skin attached to our hair follicles. These muscles control our goosebump reflex when we get cold. They help to trap heat within the hairs, keeping us from losing heat. We have no direct control over these muscles because they are under the control of the sympathetic branch of our autonomous nervous system. Within Qigong practice and internal martial arts practice, we have breath work that trains us to control these muscles and the surrounding muscles. The practitioner is told to visualise that, with every in-breath, Qi is being pulled into the skin from all over the body, and that, with every out-breath, Qi is being expelled out through the skin. Over time, the practitioner can feel their skin slightly contracting on every in-breath as if thousands of small holes are sucking in air from the surroundings, and then these holes blow out the air back into the surroundings on the out-breath. It is no surprise that practitioners of old would notice this sensation and call it 'body breathing'. They would describe and record it as breathing in Qi and breathing out Qi from the skin. They didn't have the vocabulary and anatomical understanding to explain what was happening accurately. The process of gaining some control over the muscles beneath and within the skin became known as breathing in Qi through the skin, and this was written down, taught to students and passed down through the generations.

So, if one meaning of Qi is control over these involuntary muscle systems, how do we achieve this level of control? We have all at one point or another read or been told that the Qi follows the Yi!

3

WHAT IS YI?

*B*efore we moved to the UK, my family spent a few years in Iran as refugees. During our time there, my father took a course in hypnosis. Being excited about what he was learning, he would offer to hypnotise family members and friends who would visit our home and get them to do all manner of strange and silly things. Like most young boys, wanting to emulate their father, I would listen and observe and try to practise what I had seen on myself, my brothers and my cousins. My father eventually taught me the finer points when I was a little older, and I gained some skill at self-hypnosis and hypnotising others. I even had this party trick where I could plant suggestions in awake people and make it seem like I was a mind reader when, in reality, I was repeating what I had suggested to them indirectly earlier.

One exercise that fascinated me early on was the ability to get someone to move their arm or hand without them moving it themselves in the usual way. I would watch my father tell the subject to relax and then slowly watch him direct them through active visualisation and suggestion to lift their arm up from their lap into the air. The subjects would observe their limb rise up in amazement because it felt to them like my father was moving it by magic. After a lot of pleading for him to teach me, my father explained how it was done and suggested I practise it on myself and, if it worked, I could try it on someone else. It didn't take long for me to will my own arm to move without actually engaging my arm or shoulder muscles in the usual way.

Most of our movements have been repeated so many times over the years that they feel instantaneous. We think about reaching for the remote control and, before we know it, our muscles have engaged and our arm is reaching for the remote control. Most movements are so ingrained that we don't even need to think about them. When sparring, our eyes register a punch coming at our face, our legs have already begun readjusting position, and our arms have already lifted to block and to counter.

It is possible to break down this process of movement into its component stages. We can break down the number of steps in many ways, but for our purposes we will look at movement in three steps. We will use the arm lifting from a relaxed position as an example.

> *Step 1: The first thing that occurs is the desire or the need to move the arm up. This desire may come as a response to an external stimulus or for an internal reason.*

> *Step 2: We decide that we will fulfil the desire to move and take our attention to the relevant area with the intention to complete the movement.*

> *Step 3: The voluntary muscles engage, and the arm moves in the intended way.*

It's obvious that Step 1 occurs, and then we have a choice to move on to Step 2. Most people can have Step 1 arise and then change their mind and decide to not move on to Step 2. But what isn't so obvious is that Step 2 and Step 3 are two different things and can be separated in the same way in which we can separate Steps 1 and 2. It is possible, through practice, to stop Step 3 occurring but keeping Step 2 going. We can desire to move the arm, then go to move the arm but then don't engage the muscles to move the arm. When this process is practised and refined, the arm will move anyway.

The arm moves because we allow the involuntary muscles that I described in the last chapter to move the arm. We can make this movement happen by using our mind to suggest the action, while getting the voluntary muscles out of the way. This process is a great way to understand the term 'the Yi leads the Qi', or the mind leads the involuntary muscles.

This process of intention-led movement is one of the main reasons why systems like Taijiquan are practised slowly and attentively. The practitioner needs to move in a way where they are not allowing Step 3 to occur. Students can often hear teachers telling them to "Move with intention!", instructing the students not to allow their voluntary muscles to engage, but to enable their intent to drive the movement of the involuntary muscles.

The practitioner needs to be completely present inside their body; only then can the student feel what is going on at every fleeting moment. The aim is to complete all postures without contracting the voluntary muscles, and to do that the Shen needs to be internally gathered.

4

WHAT IS SHEN?

*S*hen is one of those mystifying concepts that needs a little bit of work to explain. Shen is often described as our overall attitude; when our focus, emotions, intention and will combine, giving us a specific personality or quality of character. This understanding of Shen is not wrong and likely comes from the concept of Wu Shen or Five Shen. Wu Shen teaches that the Shen can be divided in accordance with the phases of the five elements into Shen, Yi, Po, Zhi and Hun. These phases all represent the different aspects of a person's mental and spiritual faculties. The Wu Shen theory is a complex area that gets into internal alchemy and traditional Chinese medicine and doesn't serve our immediate needs. I wanted to include a brief description of the Wu Shen above, so that it is clear that the concept of Shen is layered and, the more we explore it, the more layers we uncover. In this chapter, I want to hone in on the idea of Shen in its fire element phase; our consciousness as it expresses itself in subjective experience.

According to the theory of the Wu Shen, Shen isn't quite ours but is received from the heavenly realm; it is the divine, entering our realm and experiencing reality. This doesn't have to be a religious idea; it is an idea that alludes to the hard problem of consciousness that is currently being explored in the worlds of neuroscience and artificial intelligence. Why does it feel like something to be me, and how does this feeling arise?

The idea of Shen as is taught in Chinese internal systems is often alien to cultures that have no inner contemplative tradition. Still, anyone with some amount of meditation training or meditative prayer training can straightaway grasp what quality this word is trying to describe even if they haven't experienced it yet. In many English translations of Chinese texts, we see Shen being translated to 'Spirit', 'Heart', 'Heart-Mind', and sometimes even 'God'. These descriptions do very little to solve the mystery of what Shen actually is and still leaves the practitioner either disillusioned with the idea and discarding it or wrongly thinking that their abilities are not good enough to currently understand it so they will come back to it later, which they often don't.

So the question remains, how do we understand Shen without using other words that also need explaining? Like all things within the traditional martial arts, a real understanding of these concepts does not come from theorising but must come from doing. Our own subjective experience of the process begins to give us a level of insight that we did not have before. I want to use two different analogies to bring you closer to the flavour of what Shen is. Like most analogies, they may break down at one point. Still, they helped me formulate a coherent concept of something that is limited by concepts.

I invite you to consider the following:

When you are breathing, you are aware that you are breathing. When you are walking, you are aware that you are walking. When you are in pain, you are aware that you are in

31

pain. When you are thinking, you are aware that you are thinking. And when you are seeing, you are aware that you are seeing. Unlike concentrated awareness, which is like shining a torch on a specific thing, this open awareness or knowing is like a floodlight that permeates the whole landscape. This underlying knowing or awareness precedes and has arising in it our thoughts, our feelings, even our sense of self. This awareness is limitless and can be likened to a vast emptiness that all experience arises within.

Imagine gazing into a mirror and seeing the world reflected back at you. The seeming depth we see in the mirror, the colours and the separation of objects are all illusory. All that is present is the glass, and this glass can be likened to Shen. The rich world that we experience is not real; there is only Shen which all things arise in and are a part of, making it seem like a rich universe with depth.

Open your eyes and look at an object. You can see your body, the object and the space between, in your visual field. You may hear some noises in the background and even feel some sensation on your skin. However, is this a true reflection of the external world? The object that you see is arising in your mind, the area that you see between you and the object is arising in your mind, and your own body that you see is arising in your mind. The noise that you hear is arising in your mind, and the feeling on your skin is arising in your mind. Now don't get me wrong, I am not saying that there is no object external to you there. I'm just saying that what you are experiencing is not that external thing. It is your mind's formulation of what is there. We have no direct experience of our outer world. We only create images of our external world inside our minds. From your perception of your finger to your perception of the North Star when you look up in the sky, all exist within that space that we call 'Shen'. When one understands this, the duality of object and subject breaks down. All is contained in consciousness or Shen.

Some of you will read this and understand the idea straightaway, and some will think, what is he talking about? I apologise to the latter. Trying to explain some of these concepts is like trying to describe the colour red to someone who is blind from birth.

So, when we find terms like,

 "The shen should be internally gathered."

— (T'AI CHI CH'UAN CHING, ATTRIBUTED TO CHANG SAN-FENG [EST. 1279–1386], AS RESEARCHED BY LEE N SCHEELE)

this means that we need to bring this reflective quality of awareness inside and not attach to external distractions that arise. The instruction is advising us to shine the floodlight as much as we can on our internal condition. Only when we are intimately aware of our own internal state can we direct the Yi to mobilise the Qi.

A further point that is important to note is an instruction we often see given to practitioners regarding the Shen:

 "Suspend the crown to let the shen rise to the top of the head"

— (YANG CHENG FU'S TEN ESSENTIAL PRINCIPLES, RECORDED BY CHEN WEI MING [TRANSLATION BY PAUL BRENNAN, MARCH 2012])

Imagine you are dropped in the middle of a city square with many different roads leading off the square going in different directions. You are injured and need to get to a hospital quickly, and you know that one of these roads leads to a hospital, but you don't know which one. You can either walk blindly down each road, but you know that this will take a while, or you can float directly upwards and take a bird's-eye view of the area, seeing very quickly where you need to go.

When our awareness is externally facing, directed at a specific object or in different limbs or areas of the body, it is like pointing a small pocket mirror on that particular part but being blind to all other parts. When we can raise this awareness up and keep it in our crown and even slightly above our head, the quality of awareness shifts from a pocket mirror to a great big mirror reflecting everything to us at the same time, making all parts of our body knowable to us instantly.

Within the traditional Chinese martial arts, this triumvirate of Qi, Yi and Shen works in conjunction with the body to create a system of top-down manifestation known as the three internal harmonies:

> The Shen harmonises with the Yi
> The Yi harmonises with the Qi
> The Qi harmonies with the Body

The more refined and developed the Shen is, the clearer the awareness and insight. With clear insight, we can then guide the mind correctly and efficiently to mobilise the Qi to move the body with harmony. We practise these harmonies in the solo forms and then during partner work and eventually free sparring.

5

WHAT IS TING?

*T*ing means 'to listen', but, when instructed in kung fu systems, it doesn't mean listening with our ears. Ting means 'to listen with our body'. We can listen to our own body or listen to a partner's body through touch.

Our hands have a complex layer of fascial tissue that contains mechanoreceptors. Without getting too much into anatomical detail, mechanoreceptors in the hand sense stimuli such as touch, pressure, vibration and sound from inside our own bodies and outside our own bodies. Close your eyes and ask someone to give you an object. You will very accurately be able to create an image of the thing you are holding in your mind, without you even seeing it. Keeping your eyes closed, stand with your palms against the palms of your partner and ask them to increase the pressure, decrease the pressure, slightly take their hands to the left, slightly take their hands to the right. You will be able to tell them through touch alone in which direction they are going. This ability to sense is basic ting; the ability to listen to a partner through physical contact. Through partner drills and push hands training, we train the mind to develop the ability to create an image of a partner's forces, position in relation to us and balance. Over time, this skill becomes so natural that our brain has already deduced the shape, direction of force and structural weakness in the partner from a touch. And we have begun responding before our thinking mind has even got involved with the process.

Before a practitioner can begin developing ting in relation to a partner, a more useful pursuit is developing ting in oneself. As the old Daoist saying goes, "Understanding others is intelligence, but understanding oneself is true wisdom." These mechanoreceptors that I described above don't just exist in our hand; they are present in our fascia system that exists all over our body, close to our organs, bones and joints. I practise Brazilian Jiujitsu, when my partner gets me in a good armbar; before any pain occurs, my brain tells me that the joint is being distorted beyond what is safe, leading me to tap because I don't want to get injured. This knowing occurs because of these mechanoreceptors. As mentioned above, the secret is in training correctly. When we train to become aware of the inside of our bodies for tension, bad alignment or structural weakness, we are forcing the mechanoreceptors deeper and deeper inside our fascial web to wake up and send a picture of our internal physical state to our minds. This engagement of our mechanoreceptors gives us the ability to be present in different parts of our bodies at different depths and to see everything that is going on. We can expand this internal awareness to feel the whole body together and not just separate parts through training.

Sticking Hands or Push Hands practice is very common in traditional Chinese martial arts. One of the main benefits students get from these practices early on in their training is developing ting; this ability to understand a partner's intention through touch alone. As mentioned in the section on Yi, before we initiate a movement our involuntary muscles move in that direction. A practitioner who has a highly trained ting ability will pick up on this pre-movement and counter it. To the untrained person, it can sometimes seem like the person can read their mind, but, in reality, it's just that they picked up Step 2 of movement, as mentioned in the chapter on Yi, before Step 3 could happen.

6

WHAT IS SONG?

*C*onsider a weeping willow tree. Its branches hang down loosely, allowing gravity to draw them towards the earth. The trunk of the tree itself is strong, rooted and upright, but its softer catkins and thinner branches just hang.

Song is one of those words that has no direct translation in English. So, in its place, students are often told to "relax". Relaxation, in my opinion, is not a good translation because of the related connotations. When we relax, we put our feet up, slump on the couch or lie down on the bed. For this reason, relax does not convey the concept adequately and can lead to practitioners being too limp and weak, with no structure or shape. The words I like to use with my students are either "release" or "loosen". I am also known to use the word "song" on occasion, but I try to avoid it with beginners because I want them to understand what I am instructing.

We spend a lot of time holding tension in our muscles and joints. It is easier to notice the tension that we hold in our shoulders or our jaw. But the further away from our surface the muscle is, the more difficult it is to be able to recognise tension. Song is the process of directing our Yi or intention, through ting or listening, to song or release wherever we find tension.

Habitual tension and inflexibility is a side effect of the way we live. Our muscles and tendons are tight and hold our joints locked in place, restricting the natural freedom of movement the joint is designed to go through. Due to this tightness and chronic contraction of our muscles, it takes a specific kind of training to be able to bring our awareness into the different parts of our bodies. Contracted muscles and restricted joints work like barriers, stopping the mind from entering the area and knowing it.

Every Tuesday evening in my classes, I spend around forty minutes with my students doing deep stretching. This class is usually my least attended class. This is understandable; stretching can be painful and boring, and some may be thinking that, if they wanted to do yoga, they would sign up to a yoga class!

As I have previously mentioned, kung fu must begin with changing the body, and the first step in this journey of physical transformation is to stretch and open the body. The body needs to rediscover the full range of motion in the joints, and the ligaments must become flexible and supple. The full name of the White Crane soft form I teach is Shuang Yang Bai He Rou Ruan Quan, Frost and Sun White Crane Soft and Supple Fist; the soft and supple here referring to the state our body should be in. It is a terrible indictment of our way of life when beginners in my classes can't control or even feel their own shoulder blades. Using Song to release tension and open the joints is the beginning of a long journey, but, if you neglect this early work of opening, the journey will never progress for you.

A saying often used in the internal arts is "Bones up, muscles down". Our body can be divided into two main components: our bones, which are hard and solid and work as the framework to hold our shapes together; and our soft tissue, which includes our muscles, tendons, fascia, organs, and so on. Like the trunk of the weeping willow tree, our bones should be going up. This is achieved by imagining that the crown of the head is being suspended from above, like a chandelier. This suspension of the crown creates a stretching and opening quality in the spine upwards as if each vertebra is being gently separated from the one below it. In direct contrast, the soft tissues should be released and loosened, like the catkins on the weeping willow, drawn to the earth, hanging off the tree's central structure.

SONG KUA

As children, most of us had action figures or dolls that we played with. As a child, I was fascinated with my He-Man action figure's anatomy and would pull the legs and arms out and put them back in. What I didn't know at the time was that this would help me later to understand an essential anatomical part of my own body that is integral to correct training. The 'kua' is a Chinese term referencing an area of the body that corresponds to the inguinal crease, which comes up from the perineum region to the top of the hip bone. Going back to our He-Man action figure example, it roughly corresponds to the connection point of the inside of He-Man's leg where it inserts into his body.

Where I am from, we all squat over a hole a few times a day when we need to go to the toilet. The invention of modern toilets in the Western world has almost eliminated the need for the full squat. Almost without fail, my European students all struggle with getting into a squatting position. On the other hand, my Middle Eastern and Asian students sit in the squat naturally, often surprised that their classmates seem to find the task so difficult. The Western population's lack of squatting has led to a persistent tension and a lack of flexibility in the hips and kua region. A tight kua impedes forces from moving smoothly between the upper and lower parts of the body and restricts the smooth transfer of weight from one leg to the other.

Being able to release this habitual tension and holding in the kua is integral to whole-body integration when creating and dealing with force. When in bow and arrow stance or horse stance, be mindful of your kua region and allow gravity to act on the area without you doing anything to stop it. Allow your knees to open and release any tension into the feeling of gravity. If this is done correctly, you will notice your legs struggling to hold the position. This pain in your legs is due to the muscles in your hips no longer resisting gravity to hold you up, allowing the weight to be distributed across the body's connective tissue and fascial system. Preserving through this pain is an essential step in changing the body, and this period of body transformation is often referred to as 'eating bitterness'. When the hips and kua region have opened and released, upper and lower body can connect without hindrance, and power transfers smoothly from the legs to the upper body and vice versa.

When a practitioner has become proficient at creating this quality in the body, all movement happens through song. The ability to song and yield to the effects of gravity will, over time, give rise to different levels of understanding. A great way to practise song is through Zhan Zhuang or standing post practice, which I have detailed in the practice section later in the book.

It is important to note that the practice of song is straight out of the Buddhist playbook. Song is purely a process of letting go and abandoning all that is unnecessary. Initially, in our training, we have to start with that which is obvious and that we are aware of, like our big muscles and our joints. But, over time, we go deeper and deeper into the psyche and into who we fundamentally are. We have all built up a lifetime of bad habits, ways of thinking, emotional states and identities, and all of these have a direct effect on how our body and energy move and react. To unburden ourselves of this, we simply song.

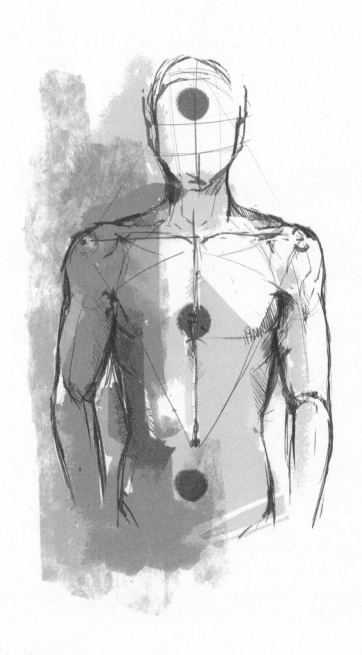

7

WHAT IS THE DAN TIAN?

*T*he dan tian is another one of those terms used repeatedly within traditional Chinese martial arts. Like most things within these traditions, the dan tian can refer to different things within different paradigms. Firstly, we need to change the question to "What are the dan tians?" because there is more than one.

1. The lower dan tian is located in the lower abdomen.
2. The middle dan tian is located in the chest.
3. The upper dan tian is located between and just above the eyebrows.

The term 'dan tian' loosely translates to 'elixir field' or 'energy centre'. The uses and functions of each one individually and then together can become quite esoteric and be the subject of several books. The dan tians used in Nei Gong and Qi Gong are more complicated and do not serve this book's objective. This chapter will discuss the lower dan tian as it pertains to the traditional Chinese martial arts.

First and foremost, the dan tian is not always present; it is an area that needs to be developed through correct training. Visualise a spherical area that fits in the area from your kua up to just below your diaphragm. On the horizontal plane, it goes from one side of your lower abdomen to the other and from the front of your body to just before your spine.

The involuntary muscle system described in the section on Qi consists of all the muscles, fascia and tendons that we have no direct control over. The lower dan tian works as a control system that links up all these different involuntary muscle systems, fascia and tendons and can control them. With training, a practitioner can identify specific paths of involuntary muscles that go from the feet to different upper body areas and vice versa; these paths are famously referred to as 'jin lu' or 'jin roads'. All these paths pass through the lower dan tian; meaning that, if we can control our lower dan tian's movements in all directions, we can control any limb or limbs' movement by just rotating the dan tian in a specific direction. This dan tian rotation causes a pull on one of these paths, leading to movement in the intended limb or limbs.

When discussing the dan tian, we should also discuss breath and how breathing works. Another thing I often heard in my early days was "make the breath and movement one". My frustration was often visible when I couldn't work out what that meant. We can use the breath in many different ways in conjunction with the dan tian. There are many other breathing methods and traditions, and they all serve a specific purpose. In the system I practise, we use reverse breathing, which is a breathing method that is often prac-tised incorrectly. When done correctly, the breath is guided by intent into the lower abdomen, down the perineum to the lower back, causing an increase in pressure in the tissues of that area. This breathing method causes the already taut jin roads to be stretched further, allowing the practitioner to better control their body through the dan tian. Of course, we can't physically breath into our lower back; we breathe into our lungs. But, by visualising the breath following the path mentioned above, and directing our intent in that specific way, we can draw our diaphragm down to a greater extent, building up the required pressure in the abdominal cavity and around the organs and involuntary muscle systems in the dan tian region.

Consider an inflated balloon. If you push your index finger into any part of it, it stretches the surrounding area, which must, to some degree, reach all the way around the balloon. Your finger in this analogy is the breath, and you can increase the pressure of the push by just pushing the finger into the balloon more. If you rotate the finger in different directions, you will see the stretch on the balloon changes in response to your finger turning. Within our body, we use the breath like the added push of the finger. It increases the abdominal cavity pressure and allows an increased degree of control over these jin roads that pass through the dan tian.

Before we can control any part of our body through our dan tian, we need to develop and control these tissue pathways that we call jin roads. We begin to do this through the three external harmonies.

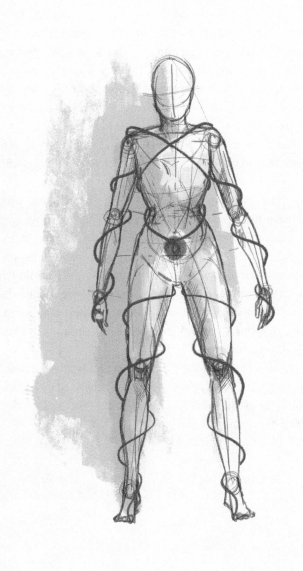

8

THE EXTERNAL HARMONIES

*H*umans like straight lines. We imagine our bodies supported by a straight spine in the same way that a ship's central mast carries the sails, spars and derricks. But the reality is, perfectly straight lines do not exist in nature. Something being perfectly straight has a disadvantage over something that can curve and bend. Anything that is perfectly straight will over time curve and bend in response to forces acting on it. If it is inflexible and rigid, it will reach its breaking point reasonably quickly and break. Perfectly straight structures are relatively weak under pressure because they have no flexibility and potential to redistribute forces across their structure through yielding.

The human body – being a product of nature – is no different; it does not have straight lines and does not move through straight lines. Our structure is wrapped in a continuous matrix of connective tissue called fascia. These fascial sheets connect our bodies from our feet to the crown of our head, stabilising our core and transferring pressure across its helix structure and distributing it across the fascial web. The Chinese medical practitioners and martial artists of old understood this. They trained the body to use this fascial structure in movement over our more obvious muscles like our biceps and triceps. When done correctly, an arm movement or a leg movement is no longer isolated to the muscles in the immediate area, but the whole body system is engaged to move the limb. We can train this method of movement to the point that closing and opening our fist is no longer an isolated hand and forearm movement but a movement that uses the fascial web that links together the hand all the way through the torso down into the feet.

The external harmonies are often described and taught in the following way:

> *The shoulders harmonise with the hips*
> *The elbows harmonise with the knees*
> *The hands harmonise with the feet*

Early on in my training, I learnt a Qigong set called Damo's Yi Jin Jing; Damo's Muscle Sinew Changing Classic. During the 6th century, a wealthy prince from India who went by the name of Tat Moh decided to renounce his status and possessions and become a Buddhist monk. Many of the wandering Buddhist monks of the time would travel to China to spread Buddhist teachings. Tat Moh arrived in a small forest that had a Buddhist monastery in it. The Mandarin for small forest is 'Shao lin'; the monastery, named after the forest, was also called Shao lin. When Tat Moh arrived, he saw that the monks living there were weak and unhealthy. They lived frugal lives and spent most of their time in meditative practices, disregarding their physical health. The legend goes that Tat Moh entered a cave and meditated for nine years looking for the solution to the problems that the monks had. At the end of the nine years, he came out with a set of exercises for the monks to practise;

these exercises would help them improve their physical health and vitality. This set of exercises have become known as the Damo (Tat Moh) Muscle Sinew Classic. The monks further developed the exercises adding martial applications to them, creating the first Shaolin kung fu style called Lohan Fist or Monk Fist. It is widely accepted that Damo's contribution was the first entry of the fascial system paradigm into Chinese martial arts. Practising Yogis in India were very familiar with this system, and it was the foundation of a lot of yoga practice.

Damo's Qi Gong set, which was possibly adapted from yoga exercises he already practised, identified a number of different channels and paths in the body that were connected and could be controlled to create movement. These channels became the basis for the meridian system in traditional Chinese medicine. These channels generally went from the top of the body to the feet through the torso. The channels on the front of the body went through the dan tian; the channels on the back of the body went through an area called the ming men. The ming men is a point located on the midline of the lower back below the spinous process of the second lumbar vertebra (L2), roughly opposite the belly button.

The dan tian and ming men area work as computers or controllers that can control the direction, strength and tautness of each of these pathways, or 'strings' as some practitioners call them. The harmonies identify the direction of these strings of tissue and how they should connect. For example, the hand connects through the elbow and shoulder, down through the torso and dan tian, going to the hip, down into the knee and into the foot. Over time, with correct training, the practitioner can control the action of the hand by instigating movement in the foot.

Some theories say that these paths connect on the same side of the body, so the left hand connects with the left foot, the left elbow with the left knee and the left shoulder with the left hip. Others say that the connection goes from one side to the other. So the left hand connects with the right foot, the left elbow with the right knee and the left shoulder with the right hip. In my experience, both are correct. These pathways in the body are so versatile that we can use the dan tian and ming men to switch sides as and when we need, depending on the intended use and circumstance.

DUI LA

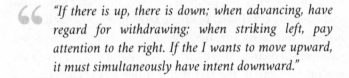

> *"If there is up, there is down; when advancing, have regard for withdrawing; when striking left, pay attention to the right. If the I wants to move upward, it must simultaneously have intent downward."*

— (T'AI CHI CH'UAN CHING, ATTRIBUTED TO CHANG
SAN-FENG [EST. 1279–1386], AS RESEARCHED BY LEE
N SCHEELE)

Dui la means to take two points away from each other or to stretch between two points. Systems that work with the external harmonies need to understand and incorporate dui la into their movements. It is surprising how often this stretching principle is not known or is ignored by kung fu practitioners. A common misunderstanding is that we need to contract and tense the arm/torso at the point of impact to transmit power into the opponent. This contraction is not correct; the type of power we aim to transmit to the opponent is hindered by tension and muscle contraction. Further to this, muscle contraction works to stop the momentum of the arm. The vibration from the sudden contraction can look very cool and powerful but it is not as damaging to an opponent as it seems.

Envision your hand with four elastic bands connecting each finger to the wrist on the palm side. Every time you open and close your palm, these bands stretch and loosen. Now envision four bands connected on the back of the hand also back down to the wrist. When the palm closes, the bands on the back of the palm stretch; when the palm opens, the bands on the front of the palm stretch. This is a crude analogy to illustrate the connections between the limbs and the dan tian but serves our purposes to show this concept of dui la. Every movement contains a stretch. So, instead of contracting and tensing on impact, which will give a kind of brittle hardness, we need to find the correct stretch in the movement. This stretching will provide us with a more taut and elastic type of hardness, and then the body will have the ability to transmit correct refined power that uses whole-body integration.

WEAPONS TRAINING

Students learn their first weapons form around two and a half to three years into their training at my kung fu school. The first weapon I teach is always the wooden staff, cut to eyebrow height. Weapons training was necessary when these kung fu systems were conceived. People needed to be able to protect themselves and their properties from bandits and invaders. But what is the point of continuing to train in weapons in the modern age?

Some people say that training with heavy weapons is an excellent way for traditional martial artists to strength train functionally, and I agree. Instead of lifting weights, a traditional martial artist will wield a heavy sword, Guan Dao, Pu Dao or spear, strengthening the joints, muscles and bones.

The practitioner learns to wield these weapons while squatting, jumping, stabbing, slicing and performing many other movements. But there is another reason that is often ignored or overlooked.

A practitioner initially trains their shape and structure to learn how to create correct lines of force through their body. They can then mobilise refined power using intention to be able to affect an opponent. Introducing a weapon into one's training allows the practitioner to integrate the weapon into their shape and structure. In essence, the weapon they are wielding becomes an extension of the body, allowing the practitioner to send intention and refined power to the tip of the staff or the sword or the spear. Every inch of the weapon is connected to the practitioner's centre and then the floor through the correct structure that has been trained.

When a practitioner reaches this level of skill, they can project their intention to the end of a one-handed or two-handed weapon. When they are seizing or locking an opponent's limb, the practitioner can instantly make the opponent's body a part of their structure in the same way as is done with a weapon. The practitioner can then attack the opponent directly at any point in the opponent's body. This process is what is meant when Chinese martial artists say that they are projecting their Qi into an opponent's joint or limb.

9

SINK THE QI

*F*or beginners, an adequate explanation of sink the Qi is to bend the knees and lower the centre of gravity. But when a practitioner's training progresses, this explanation is not enough. This instruction keeps the practitioner focused on moving the body's external shape up and down, which does not explain what is meant by sink the Qi.

Consider an hourglass. When it is tipped over, the sand in the top bulb sinks down into the bottom bulb. The more sand that sinks down into the bottom bulb, the more stable it becomes because it is no longer top-heavy but becomes bottom-heavy. When the practitioner sinks the Qi properly, it is not the shape of the body or the structure that is sinking. The sinking is happening on the inside of the body. So how does one sink the Qi? Let's begin by looking at the word 'sink'.

Sinking occurs when gravity is the dominant force acting on an object. All other forces that may oppose gravity have less magnitude and, the more these opposing forces are reduced, the faster an object will sink. Gravity is ever-present, so, to sink the Qi, the practitioner has to do nothing with their physical body apart from hold the structure in place. The practitioner will just let go or song the soft tissue while keeping the bones in the correct alignment so that the integrity of the shapes of the chosen practice is not compromised. If the practitioner can add Yi or intention to their letting go, they have come a long way to understanding what sink the Qi means. When I sink the Qi, my insides feel like grains of sand falling downwards as far as I choose to take it with my Yi or intention.

Sinking the Qi leads to filling, just like filling a glass with water begins at the bottom of the glass and gradually fills to the top. Over time, our body becomes full and can rebound, redirect and disperse external forces applied to it.

While sinking the Qi, it is essential not to forget the instruction to "sink the Qi and suspend the crown" or "muscles down and bones up". Sinking the Qi without suspending the crown will cause a collapse of the structure, and suspending the crown without sinking will cause a top-heavy structure that has no root or any real internal power. It is not uncommon to see older kung fu practitioners with very bad postures. This is often due to these practitioners ignoring the instruction to suspend the crown.

Another essential point to note here is a phrase that I have heard thousands of times shouted at me in my early days, and I am also guilty of shouting it at my students: "Get lower in your stance; bend your knees!" The first part of the statement is sound, but the best way to sink in one's stance is not for the practitioner to bend their knees but to hinge at the hips. Hinging at the hips in the same way as attempting to sit down on a stool or chair helps the shoulders and chest to release through the external harmonies of the shoulders and hips. This way of sinking in the stance will aid in the practitioner's attempts to sink the Qi.

Sinking the Qi has another significant physiological

benefit: it helps settle the fight or flight response. When we feel under threat, we tighten up, we have a feeling of rising up into our chest, shoulders and head, our breathing becomes shallower, and we lose that clarity of mind that is open, aware and settled. Blood flows to our muscles, and we are ready to do what it takes to survive. Allowing ourselves to settle back down into our lower body, we can remain calm and grounded during stressful situations and act in a more skilful way than we would have if we were reacting from a place of heightened stress.

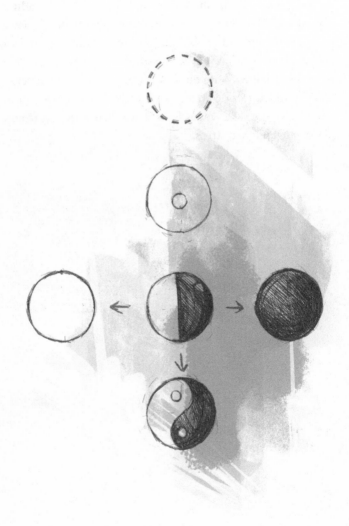

10

YIN YANG

*I*t is evident that kung fu is steeped in Daoist and Buddhist lore. One crucial aspect that is present in almost all of these arts is the concept of Yin Yang. Yin Yang won't be a new idea to most Westerners; these words have entered the zeitgeist and are often used to describe a wide range of ideas. Yin Yang has uses in Nei Gong, Qi Gong and traditional Chinese medicine. In fact, by virtue of the idea it is trying to convey, Yin Yang can be found in all things. For the purposes of this chapter, I will explain its intended meaning as it pertains to kung fu training. Before I can get into that, here is an introductory lesson on Daoist cosmology; how the I-Ching (Book of Changes) envisioned the creation and development of the universe.

In the beginning, before time, there was nothing. This nothingness or emptiness is impossible to conceive because, as humans, we think and experience the world relatively. Something is only empty in contrast with something being full. There is only nothing when we can understand something. The nothingness alluded to here is a limitless, infinite nothingness that preceded any something. Daoists called this state 'Wuji'. Wuji has several different translations but, for our purposes 'limitless' will suffice.

For some reason, unknowable by us, something arose within Wuji. Daoists call this the first appearance of Yang energy. Yang is representative of movement, expansion and heat. The laws of our universe dictate that, if something exists, so must its opposite. Newton's third law tells us that every action has an equal and opposite reaction. Yang energy cannot exist on its own in a dualistic universe. As Yang began spiralling outwards, at the same instant, Yin arose to be its opposite and spiral inwards. The interplay between Yin and Yang is called 'Taiji'. Taiji is a philosophical and metaphysical concept that should not be confused with the kung fu system called Taijiquan.

Suppose we take Taijiquan, which is supposed to be a physical manifestation of the above principle. We can see that the Taijiquan form begins in Wuji stance, which is empty of duality. The practitioner descends, pouring their weight into one leg, causing the other leg to simultaneously be empty, thus creating Yin Yang in the stance. The postures throughout the Taijiquan form represent the interplay between Yin and Yang and, at the end of the form, Yin and Yang cease, ascending back into Wuji. A Taijiquan form can be likened to a physical representation of the universe from its creation to its end.

The Wuji stance is not the only representation of Yin Yang within kung fu principles. Any two opposing principles within the body show the interplay between Yin Yang. The upper and lower body, the left and right side of the body, even the front and back of the body. One fundamental principle that is a foundational concept is opening and closing.

When a practitioner begins to get some basic proficiency

in their kung fu training, they begin to view all postures as either opening or closing; opening being expansive movements away from the centre of the body and closing being movements that contract in towards the centre. The practitioner then begins to string these series of openings and closings together, moving from open and close and back to open smoothly and harmoniously. But, as the practitioner progresses, they realise that it is not that straightforward. They find postures which have half the body opening and the other half closing. They go on to realise that the opening and closing are not one after the other after all. The opening movements must give rise to the closing movements, and the closing movements must give rise to the opening movements. Another realisation that eventually occurs is that they can feel the fascia and front of the body pulling them back to close at maximum open. When open is at its maximum, the potential for close is evident. At maximum close, fascia in the back of the body are pulling the practitioner's structure back to open; when close is at its maximum the potential for open is evident. This quality is not unlike the symbol of Taiji. Within maximum Yang, we have the seed for Yin and, within maximum Yin, we have the seed for Yang.

Movement, stillness and power can also be looked at in terms of Yin Yang. Taiji theory teaches us that we can arrive at a condition if we take its opposite all the way to its zenith. Just like if we keep walking east relative to where we are we will eventually end up west of where we started. This theory is a teaching in kung fu systems that is often ignored or not even understood.

To understand skilful, correct movement in the context of our arts, we need to begin practising true stillness. Because it is only through profound levels of stillness that can one begin to understand how to move correctly. In the same vein, to understand how to issue real power, we need to let go of our current understanding of power (which is muscular strength) and cultivate its opposite: relaxing and releasing.

So, seek stillness in the midst of motion and find what moves when one is still!

11

THE THIRTEEN WONDERS

I have spent the past two decades training in and teaching a system that is heavily influenced by the White Crane system of Yongchun, Fujian Province, China. The system I practise is known as Tiger Crane Combination, heavily influenced by Yongchun White Crane and Taizuquan; the style developed by emperor Taizu of the Song dynasty. We use the word 'tiger' because Taizuquan heavily influenced many tiger styles developed in southern China.

Our fourth syllabus form is Shi San Tai Bao. Shi San Tai Bao translates to 'the Thirteen Wonders' and is a White Crane form found in some Yongchun White Crane lineages from Fuzhou. This form is unique and indicates that, unlike many of its counterparts, the White Crane system has the full internal picture. The White Crane system understands how the internal dynamics create power without the need for muscular strength in the conventional sense. The Thirteen Wonders is a term used to describe the Eight Gates and the Five Elements.

THE EIGHT GATES

The Eight Gates are most commonly called Peng, Lu, Ji, An, Cai, Lie, Zhou and Kao, and they describe the different ways in which we can manipulate and direct an opponent's force, and the various ways in which we can apply force to an opponent. Different systems call these names different things, but they all mean the same thing. For example, in the Southern Crane system I practise, we learn a form called San Zhan or Sum Chien right at the start. One important thing that this form teaches us is the principles of Float, Swallow, Spit and Sink, which correspondents to Peng, Lu, Ji and An.

Here is a breakdown of the Eight Gates, or eight ways to use and manipulate force when applied to a partner or when a partner applies the force on the practitioner.

PENG

Peng is often translated as 'to ward off'. When using Peng, the practitioner creates fullness and expansion, causing the opponent to lose their root to the ground, causing them to float on the exterior of the practitioner's body. An opponent applies a force on to the practitioner. The practitioner, on feeling the contact, through highly trained ting and correct structure, will aim to lead the opponent's direction of force through their structure to the floor. The corresponding force that bounces back off the floor will uproot the opponent.

Without Peng, the other forces will not work. Peng can only come about after the practitioner has developed their shape correctly, achieved an adequate level of song and ting and has sunk the Qi. When all this is correct, and a partner pushes you, it is like they are pushing against a tree. They can't find your centre and, the more they push, the more they uproot themselves.

LU

Lu can be translated as 'to roll back'. When using Lu, you are emptying the area that is being pushed, which causes your opponent to feel like they are being swallowed into the space you have emptied. An opponent applies a force on to the practitioner; the practitioner yields to their force, just enough to see if the opponent will continue their push. If the opponent continues their direction of force, the practitioner will continue leading the opponent into emptiness, causing the opponent to overcommit and eventually lose their balance.

Lu is achieved through firstly having correct Peng, good ting and good hip rotation to lead the opponent into emptiness. When a partner pushes you, and you use Lu correctly, the opponent will feel like they are just millimetres away from grasping your centre, but, for some reason, it keeps alluding them. In their attempts to find your centre, the opponent will eventually overcommit and lose their root.

JI

Ji is often translated as 'to press' or 'to squeeze'. This doesn't mean that you are pressing or squeezing your opponent; it means that you are pressing or squeezing their force into as small a point as possible. The human nervous system likes stability, so, when an opponent pushes, they want to feel a good grip on the ground beneath their feet, and a good palm or two placed on the person they are pushing. When an opponent applies a force on to the practitioner, the practitioner uses ting to know the direction of the force and then squeezes the opponent's force into a smaller point than the opponent is comfortable with. This causes the opponent to lose their stability and collapse underneath the ever-present Peng coming back at them from their own force.

Ji can be likened to pushing a giant open book. As you push the book from the inside, on either side of the spine of the book, the book begins to close, causing your force to squeeze into a tighter and tighter space until you collapse.

AN

An translates as 'to push'. When using An, the practitioner is looking for the part of the opponent that is empty, and putting force into it, to see how they will react. Whenever an opponent applies a force, they will usually be using a specific body part to apply the force, while having another body part helping to hold the structure in place. With An, the practitioner feels which part of the opponent's body is integral to the opponent's structure and directs force there. The opponent's structure will either collapse or change to readjust, leaving them open for attack during their attempts to find balance.

With An, the force feels like pressure being applied from above them, causing them to compress. As the partner's body naturally wants to decompress or change, the practitioner can then change direction and uproot the opponent.

CAI

Cai means 'to pluck' or 'to pull' an opponent off their root. The practitioner pulls on the opponent to see how they react. If the opponent yields and follows, the practitioner has to also follow and change. If the opponent reacts by tensing up, they can be attacked.

LIE

Lie means 'to split' or 'to break'. The opponent is pulled into the practitioner's spiral and is either sucked down or thrown out. The practitioner takes the opponent in different directions, to open them up to attack, to throw them out, to break a limb or to lock or seize a joint.

ZHOU

Zhou means 'to attack' the opponent with an elbow. The opponent presses against the forearm and finds that it yields. Excited to enter, they run into the practitioner's elbow. It is essential to understand which part yields and which part doesn't.

KAO

Kao is often translated as 'to shoulder', but it describes the energy of a lean. The practitioner leans into the opponent's centre of gravity to see how they will react. Does he resist, yield or get stuck?

The Eight Gates are often associated with the eight trigrams of the I-Ching. A small explanation of this can help the practitioner understand the quality or feel of each of these forces and how they differ from each other.

In the section on Yin Yang, I briefly explained how Yin Yang arises from Wuji. A solid horizontal line often symbolises Yang and a broken horizontal line Yin. These two symbols become four symbols showing the different possible variations of these symbols together. These four symbols further multiply to become eight symbols, showing the different variations of these symbols together. These eight symbols of the different combinations of Yin and Yang are called the eight trigrams or 'Bagua'.

Working with the four main gates, Peng, Lu, Ji and An, we can see how the correspondences with the trigrams give us a clue as to the force's quality or feel.

Peng corresponds with three solid lines or three Yang lines. This shows us that Peng should feel like Yang at its maximum; full, expansive and inflated. An opponent cannot overpower this quality as much as they try.

Lu, on the other hand, corresponds with three broken lines or three Yin lines. This shows us that Lu should feel like Yin at its maximum; empty and yielding, with no force of its own. An opponent cannot find anything to grasp on to when they apply force and, the more they look for something to push, the deeper they fall into the emptiness.

Ji corresponds to two broken lines surrounding a solid line, or two Yin lines surrounding a Yang line; seeming soft on the outside but with a hard, strong centre. An opponent feels squeezed into the centre with nowhere to go but into the needle hidden in the cotton.

An corresponds to two solid lines surrounding a broken line, or two Yang lines surrounding a Yin line. In contrast to Ji, An feels solid but has a softer, less insistent, centre. The opponent feels crushed under the seeming weight of An, but, because of its soft centre, if the opponent gives the slightest hint of change, An changes first.

We add the five steps or directions of advance, retreat, turn left, turn right and central equilibrium to the Eight Gates to form the Thirteen Wonders. This is another way of saying that the Eight Gates can be applied in five different directions or steps. All principles in kung fu systems that use the Thirteen Wonders are based on the interplay of these forces and directions of movement.

FA JIN - DISCHARGING POWER

*S*ometimes we see videos online of kung fu practitioners doing partner work that seems so out there; seemingly defying the laws of physics that many people consider it as another example of fake traditional martial arts. An example that is often seen is when a student touches their instructor on the arm or the torso and, without much perceptible movement, the student jumps back as if he has received an electric shock. Some sceptics quickly claim that it is fake, and the instructor and student are in on it together. Other sceptics are a little more charitable and claim that it is not fake but is an example of subconscious suggestion. I'm sure that there are fake examples and examples that rely on suggestion, but there are a few genuine examples, and I'll explain how it works.

The human nervous system is wired for survival. In every action it performs, the subconscious mind has a prediction of any reaction already programmed in. When this expected reaction or feedback doesn't happen, the nervous system seizes up or attempts to correct itself by getting out of the situation. We have all at one point or another walked down some stairs and missed a step. The mind goes blank for a second, and the body reacts without our control. When a student pushes on their teacher's body, the student's nervous system expects to meet some resistance or push back. But the teacher, with impeccable timing, does the opposite. They yield ever so slightly to neutralise the incoming force. The student, expecting to meet resistance at the culmination of their push, instead finds emptiness, as if they have pushed against a heavy door only to find it disappear just as they are bracing to give maximum power. The more momentum the student puts into their push, the more their body will feel like it is falling. The nervous system corrects this by counter-acting the danger of falling by throwing the body in the opposite direction. The teacher can then add a little push of his own through his correct and trained structure, and the student goes flying back. The more a teacher does this with a student, the more the student's nervous system is conditioned to react in a certain way. This is why it is always easier to get the best effects on your own students who have done this exercise before.

This process is described in the following classic:

> "Let the opponent attack with great force; use four ounces to deflect a thousand pounds. Attract to emptiness and discharge."
>
> — (SONG OF PUSH HANDS BY UNKNOWN AUTHOR, AS RESEARCHED BY LEE N SCHEELE)

This above process is just one way in which some of the more physics-defying techniques are achieved by kung fu practitioners. A student pushing an instructor in a straight line, committing to the push and waiting to be uprooted, will probably never happen in such a sanitised way in a real fight.

But drilling this exercise is essential because it helps develop the correct timing, sensitivity and structure to do some version of it when attacked more randomly. When an attacker comes in to grapple or take you down, you might be able to take their root for a second or two, giving you an advantage. But of course, you have to have trained with an uncooperative partner, and have practised using this skill during free sparring. A practitioner can't expect to practise forms and push hands and know how to fight; that's not how it works. Forms will make you great at forms; push hands will make you great at push hands. To get good at fighting, you need to train at fighting. It's as simple as that.

II

PRACTISE

13

ZHAN ZHUANG

*V*ery early on in my training, I was introduced to Zhan Zhuang practice. At the age of sixteen, I just wanted to learn to fight, but I was instead forced to stand for sustained periods with legs bent and arms held out in a circle in front of me. I was told to relax and breathe and just be in the present. The pain in my shoulders, legs and back would quickly become unbearable, and the instruction to relax felt like a cruel joke. At the time, my instructor called it the greater meditation position, but this may have been him just repeating what he was taught because Zhan Zhuang is not meditation, and words matter.

Zhan Zhuang or standing post practice is seen by some as a fundamental practice that should not be neglected, but some don't hold it in the same esteem and teach it only as an auxiliary exercise. In my own training, standing post practice over the past two decades has helped transform my body and mind in profound ways. I teach it as an essential fundamental practice. If practised correctly, the forms will help you achieve the same things that the standing practice will help you achieve, but, in my opinion, incorporating the standing practice will help get you there much faster.

Within the White Crane system that I practise and teach, we have several standing postures that are designed to change your body and mind. These static postures help you align your structure correctly, allow your flesh to loosen and song down, find the solidity of the earth and allow that solidity to fill the space created by sinking the Qi, leading to Peng: the fundamental force of the Eight Gates. In the process of this practice, the practitioner develops their ability to ting or listen to their internal state, the ability to direct Yi or intent and the ability to stay balanced and in equilibrium

———

Here is one of the standing postures that I teach, which you can practise to develop an excellent internal foundation. The posture is called three circle standing.

> *Step 1: Feet parallel, at shoulder width, bend your
> knees so that, if you look down, you can't see
> your toes, and allow your knees to push out
> slightly as if you have a big ball between your
> knees.*

> *Step 2: Hinge at your hips, as if you are going to sit
> down on a bar stool, allow your tailbone to roll
> under, get rid of the arch in the lower back,
> straightening your lumbar spine.*

Step 3: Suspend the crown of your head, imagine something gently pulling up the crown of your head – this should allow you to create space in your spine – and tuck in your chin slightly to straighten the cervical spine.

Step 4: Hold your arms in front of your body in a circle as if you are holding a ball and presenting it to someone. Your elbows should be sunk, and index fingers about chin height.

Step 5: While in the posture, your job is to scan through your body, looking for muscle contraction and tension and releasing as much as possible without losing the above shape. Start at the top of your body and release tension, then go to the next part and release tension. Keep repeating this process until the end of your standing session.

Different teachers instruct different durations for standing. Some say hours, and others say that five minutes is enough. In my experience, this depends on the practitioner. The exercise is only effective when the above rules are followed. As soon as you get tired or your mind wanders, it's better to stop, because continuing to hold the posture won't work in the way it is supposed to and won't be developing what the exercise is supposed to be developing. Saying this, we should always attempt to push a little more than we are physically able, as this will help us get stronger and develop the body correctly.

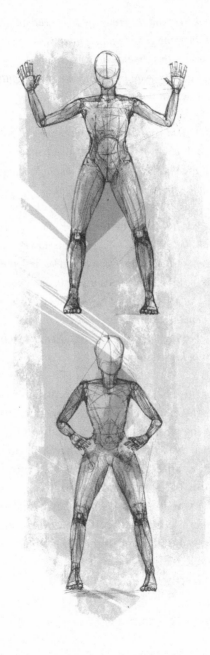

14

WHITE CRANE FLAPS

The White Crane Flaps exercises are a set of foundation exercises designed to help the body develop and move correctly. These exercises are part of the White Crane system's foundation training. For those of you who are familiar with the Song Gong or loosening exercises of Master Huang Sheng Shyan's Yang Style Taijiquan, the White Crane Flaps exercises are, in my opinion, what inspired master Huang to develop them. Master Huang was a Fujian White Crane practitioner for many years before he began training Yang Style Taijiquan with Master Cheng Man-Ch'ing.

I will explain how you can practise two of the White Crane Flaps exercises here. Among other things, both are designed to help your body understand how to connect the external harmonies during movement.

WHITE CRANE FLAPS EXERCISE 1

Step 1: Feet parallel, at shoulder width, bend your knees so that, if you look down, you can't see your toes. Your knees should be directly above your big toes.

Step 2: Hinge at your hips, as if you are going to sit down on a bar stool, allow your tailbone to roll under get rid of the arch in the lower back, straightening your lumbar spine.

Step 3: Suspend the crown of your head, imagine something gently pulling up the crown of your head. This should allow you to create space in your spine, and tuck in your chin slightly to straighten the cervical spine.

Step 4: Spread your arms out, palms either side of your head, in line with your nose, with your palms facing forward, thumbs at ear height and shoulders settled, as if the police are asking you to put your hands up.

Step 5: Visualise a flat surface in front of you at naval height and close the front of your body, drawing your shoulders forward, allowing your elbows to sink and come together causing your palms to move towards the imaginary surface to strike. At the same time as your arms descend, your legs should straighten to about 90 per cent straight.

Step 6: Draw your arms back up to the starting position and sink back down in your stance by hinging at your hips. Repeat as many times as you like.

WHITE CRANE FLAPS EXERCISE 2

Repeat Steps 1 through 4 to get into the starting position.

Step 5: Do the same arm movement and rising and sinking in the stance as the first exercise, but one arm at a time, alternating arms on each repetition. Repeat as many times as you like.

These exercises are designed to be very simple to remember and to do. But don't be fooled. The White Crane Flaps exercises are layered and, the more you practise it correctly, the more insight you will get into the internal connections and lines of power in your body.

15

ASTRAL BODY METHOD

One day, I was training with Kristina, my wife, in the kitchen. The kids were playing on their own and not demanding their mum's attention. Kristina expressed her frustration that she didn't understand what I meant when I instructed her to do her forms, not by moving her muscles in the normal way, but by allowing her mind or intention to move her. She explained that, if she stands still and tries to use her mind to move, nothing happens. I understood her frustration because some of my students had the same problem. In my attempts to explain how I do it, the proverbial lightbulb turned on in my head, and I told her to try something new. When she tried it, it immediately worked for her; she was able to move her limbs by directing her intention. She even had some luck controlling my balance when she incorporated the method into our push hands practice. I taught this method to some of my students, and they have all had success with it. I decided to call it the Astral Body Method.

The idea is straightforward. All you have to do is imagine that you have an astral body or ghost body superimposed over your normal body.

> *Step 1: Stand in the correct posture and shape of whatever system you practise. Make sure you are relaxed and are not holding tension in your muscles.*

> *Step 2: Visualise an astral body superimposed over your normal body, and imagine that you have the same level of control over your astral body as you have over your normal body.*

> *Step 3: When you want to move your arms in any direction, move your astral arm instead of your normal arm. When you want to move your body in any direction, move your astral body instead of your normal body.*

This method should help you quickly develop your ability to control your body through intention. You can practise the same thing with a partner touching your arm. When you move your astral arm while someone is touching it, it should cause a reaction in your partner's structure and balance.

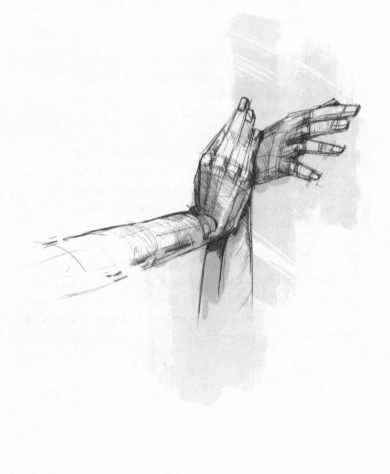

16

BUTTERFLY ON LOTUS FLOWER PARTNER EXERCISE

*T*his exercise is one of my favourite exercises to help introduce students to touch sensitivity. We are often told that a master in the traditional arts can read an opponent's intention before the opponent moves. This skill can often sound quite mysterious and slightly supernatural. But in reality, it doesn't have to be. As I explained in the section on ting, we can sense an opponent's direction and magnitude of movement through the mechanoreceptors in the fascia. This exercise helps to hone and refine this skill.

For this exercise, you will need a partner.

BUTTERFLY ON LOTUS FLOWER SINGLE PALM

Step 1: Get your partner to place one of their arms out, palm down. You then place one of your palms very lightly on to the back of their hand.

Step 2: Your partner begins moving around, smoothly, going left, going right, going up, going down, in any order that they want. It is your job to keep your palm touching their hand, trying not to lose contact.

Step 3: When you have become comfortable with the exercise, the person following can practise it with their eyes closed.

Do this for five minutes on each hand.

BUTTERFLY ON LOTUS FLOWER TWIN PALM

Step 1: Get your partner to place both of their arms out, palms down. You then place both of your palms very lightly on to the back of their hands.

Step 2: Your partner begins moving around, smoothly, going left, going right, going up, going down, in any order that they want. It is your job to keep your palms touching their hands, trying not to lose contact.

Step 3: When you have become comfortable with the exercise, the person following can practise it with their eyes closed.

Over time, as you get more competent at the exercise, you can ask your partner to move faster with more sudden changes in direction. The twin palm method is more difficult, so, if you are new to touch sensitivity training, don't skip the single palm practice.

17

MEDITATION

I decided to include a chapter on meditation, simply because the higher aims of the traditional Chinese martial arts outside of combat has always been awakening or enlightenment, and it helps in experiencing the nature of Shen. If you have been training the traditional arts for a long time, and your thoughts are still mainly about violence, I don't think you have truly explored the higher lessons these arts have to teach. The Wudang Mountain martial arts developed out of Daoist philosophy, and they embody these principles within the arts. The Shaolin martial arts were developed from exercises taught by Bodhidharma, a wandering Buddhist monk, who was probably an expert in Indian yoga exercises. The traditional arts are a vehicle for the practitioner to gain insight into the true nature of self and reality.

Some kung fu systems are called 'moving meditation exercises'. They help focus the mind, cultivate non-attachment and train the mind to be here and now, present in the body and not lost in the narrative of self that is always running. During practice, the mind quietens down, and complete awareness is on the internal state, in the present moment. A flaw is noticed in the posture; the mind attaches to it and is no longer in the present moment. Noticing this disturbance to the present moment and coming back to the present is the great work.

I remember the first time during a meditation session when I had a small glimpse of my mind's true nature. I spent three months doing daily one-hour meditation sessions. Most were frustrating; I couldn't concentrate on my breath for very long before I got distracted, by postural pain, or the ticking of the clock or pins and needles in my legs. On this occasion, I had all the usual frustrating distractions arise, but, instead of allowing it to mess with my state of mind, I used each distraction as a point of meditation, I just transferred my focus to the thing that was trying to get my attention and observed it, without judging it or being annoyed by it. Suddenly my perspective changed. I was no longer the distraction, or the person being distracted; I was the space that all this occurred in.

VIPASSANA - INSIGHT MEDITATION

My favourite meditation method and the one I have had the most success with is insight meditation, known as Vipassana. Vipassana translates from the Pali into 'insight' and is more commonly known in the West as mindfulness meditation. Vipassana is a method for the practitioner to gain insight into the workings of his or her own mind. I have students who come to me after attempting this form of meditation and complain that they don't find it relaxing or calming at all. It frustrates them because they cannot stop themselves from getting distracted. I tell them the following: this form of meditation isn't about relaxing or calming the mind; it's merely about observing the mind's erratic nature and how it can't be still, how it jumps from one thing to another constantly. To be able to observe our mind so closely without attaching and being carried off by any of its projections, we need to hone and strengthen our concentration, and this takes effort and time. Insight meditation is hard work but worth it. Try it yourself daily and see what you uncover.

The Method

> *Step 1: Sit down in a comfortable position, posture upright and body relaxed.*

> *Step 2: Take a few deep breaths to settle into yourself and close your eyes. Begin by noticing your buttocks and your legs against the object you are sitting on. Notice your clothes against your skin and notice any bodily sensations that arise.*

> *Step 3: Bring your concentration to your breath going in and out. (Make sure you don't get caught up in trying to control the breath or directing it in any way or form. Just observe it, like you would observe a candle flame flickering in the breeze.) You can observe the breath wherever it feels most natural. Some people concentrate on the lifting and dropping of their abdomen; some on the feeling of the air brushing against the sides of their nostrils as they inhale and exhale. Choose what works for you but stick to one method.*

Step 4: You will inevitably be drawn away from your breath by thoughts, noises or other sensations in your body. When this happens, please don't allow this to annoy you or cause frustration, but allow your concentration to focus on these new stimuli and observe it until it passes and then come back to the breath.

Step 5: When you notice that you are caught in thought, and are no longer on the breath, bring yourself back to the breath without frustration or annoyance.

Step 6: Do this for as long as you like. It can be 5 minutes or 1 hour. It's up to you.

Insight meditation is one of the easiest methods one can begin to use, and, at the same time, one of the most challenging methods to do correctly and sustain over a period of time. When doing this method of awareness practice, you will very quickly begin to see the reactive nature of your mind and how quickly it attaches to every stimulus that it is given.

Like all exercise, with meditation the key is consistency. Doing it once or twice will do nothing for you. Doing it consistently will allow you to build up the momentum to gain insight into your mind and help you achieve a state of equanimity; a state of mind undisturbed by thoughts or feelings in any direction.

EPILOGUE

A student went to his meditation teacher and said,
  "My meditation is horrible! I feel so distracted, or
  my legs ache, or I'm constantly falling asleep. It's
  just horrible!"
"It will pass," the teacher said matter-of-factly.
A week later, the student came back to his teacher.
  "My meditation is wonderful! I feel so aware, so
  peaceful, so alive! It's just wonderful!'
"It will pass," the teacher replied matter-of-factly.

My Tiger Crane teacher would hold seminars over the summer, where we would spend a weekend at his home in Kent training the hard and soft elements of our system. On one of these occasions, we had spent the morning working on Qi cultivation exercises, body sensitivity and breath-work. In the afternoon while we were working on our White Crane soft form, my body felt as though it was as light as a feather and full of energy. I could create the feeling of energy flow and heat in any limb on command. I could not contain my excitement. I was sure that I had finally attained a high skill level. I spent the whole day recreating the feeling at will and telling others at the seminar how great I felt. The following day, as much as I tried, I could not recreate the previous day's feelings and sensations. This caused me a lot of frustration and distress. I couldn't understand why I had lost the ability to control my energy flow, leaving me disappointed and dejected for weeks.

Our training journey in the world of kung fu, starting from our first day as a beginner up to the day we bid farewell, involves a complete transformation of body and mind. This process of transformation will manifest in a multitude of different ways, ranging from physical and emotional pain all the way to developing abilities that can seem supernatural. One of the traps that we all fall into at some point in our training journey is that we attach to these manifestations as if they are the goal. How a particular exercise or training method feels and the sensations or abilities that may arise are important markers on the journey, but attaching to them and trying to recreate them keeps us static, not allowing us to advance.

When training in your chosen system, pay detailed attention to the instructions given by your teacher because this is the only thing you need to recreate. Any feelings, sensations or abilities that arise from implementing the instructions can be noted and put aside. Achieving mastery in traditional kung fu hinges on how well you can implement the causes and not attach to the effects.

ABOUT THE AUTHOR

Shkar Sharif is the founder and head instructor at Kung Fu Zone, a traditional Chinese martial arts school based in the UK, specialising in the Tiger Crane Combination Kung Fu system and the White Crane Soft Fist known as Shuang Yang. In addition to the Southern Crane system, Shkar trains in Yang Style Taijiquan and Brazilian Jiujitsu and has more than 25 years of experience in the martial arts, studying and teaching in Asia, Europe and the Middle East.

From a young age, Shkar was drawn to the spiritual and the mystical and has trained in and explored several traditions that have helped him understand what the masters of old were alluding to in their lessons. In addition to studying philosophy, Shkar has trained in Sufi mysticism, Vipassana and Dzogchen meditation, and has been initiated into several Hermetic traditions. Shkar's training in these traditions has given him a unique insight into the more transformative aspects of traditional Chinese martial arts.

Made in the USA
Coppell, TX
07 September 2021

61956291R00059